I0490568

BUSINESS LESSONS FROM DRUG CARTEL LORDS

By Dr. Javnyuy Joybert

BUSINESS LESSONS FROM DRUG CARTEL LORDS:

17 Lessons To Learn & Execute

By Dr. Javnyuy Joybert

By Dr. Javnyuy Joybert

TABLE OF CONTENTS

INTRODUCTION

Business Lessons from the Drug Cartel Lords is a thought-provoking book that delves into the world of drug cartels and the strategies they use to run their organizations. The author, a long-time observer of drug cartels through watching of documentaries and movies, noticed that these criminal organizations employ some of the most intelligent and effective strategies to succeed in their illicit activities.

The book is a result of the author's fascination with the inner workings of drug cartels, and the desire to understand how these strategies can be adapted for use in legitimate businesses. The author has carefully studied drug cartel movies and documentaries, particularly those from Eastern Europe and South America, and has gained valuable insights into the recruitment, manufacturing, delivery, and influence of these criminal organizations.

The book is organized into chapters that focus on specific strategies used by drug cartels, such as recruiting, organizing, and motivating a team, building a network of contacts, and maintaining a low profile. The author not only explains these strategies but show how they can be adapted for use in legitimate businesses. I know the question running through your mind now is, what are drug cartels ?

Drug cartels are those criminal groups that deal with illegal drugs. They have their roots in Mexico. It all started around the early 1900s, when a group of farmers in the state of Sinaloa began growing and selling marijuana and opium. As more and more people in the United States wanted these drugs, the cartels began to expand their operations and smuggle large amounts of drugs across the border. Over time, they got bigger and more powerful, and even created networks of traffickers and corrupt officials to help them out. They also started getting involved in other criminal activities, like money laundering and extortion. And unfortunately, drug cartels still exist today and continue to be a major problem in Mexico and other Latin American countries.

This book is a must-read for anyone interested in understanding the inner workings of criminal organizations and how their strategies can be adapted for use in legitimate businesses. The book is written in an easy-to-understand style that will help readers understand the concepts discussed. Whether you are a business owner, an entrepreneur, or just someone interested in learning more about the strategies used by drug cartels, this book is a valuable resource.

By Dr. Javnyuy Joybert

CHAPTER 1

MASTER PHYSICAL SKILLS TO BE IN THE GAME (PUNCHES, SWORDS & GUNS)

IN watching drug cartel movies, including films that depict real life stories, I have noticed a common thread among drug lords: they are all proficient in hand-to-hand combat, sword fighting, gun usage, and other forms of weaponry. This is because the drug business is incredibly ruthless, with fierce competition and constant threats to one's power and territory. Simply having a team of bodyguards is not enough to protect oneself and maintain control in this cutthroat industry.

By Dr. Javnyuy Joybert

It is not just in the drug world where this type of physical prowess is necessary. The same can be said for the business world. In order to truly succeed as an entrepreneur, it is crucial to have a deep understanding and mastery of the core technical skills that drive your industry. For example, if you run a software development agency, it would greatly benefit you as CEO to have a strong background in coding and technology development. This allows you to not only lead and manage your team effectively, but also to have a hands-on understanding of the products and services you are offering to customers.

As an entrepreneur, it is important to take responsibility for mastering the hard skills that are essential to your business. Do not rely solely on your team to possess all the necessary knowledge and expertise. Instead, take the initiative to learn and improve upon the skills that are crucial to the success of your company. This will not only give you a competitive edge, but it will also instill confidence in your team, investors and customers, knowing that the leader of the company is fully competent and capable.

Additionally, it's important to note that in the drug cartels, violence and intimidation are often used as means of control and power maintenance. However, this is not a sustainable or ethical way to run a business. Instead, entrepreneurs should focus on building a strong reputation and fostering trust with customers, employees and partners. This can be achieved through transparent and honest business practices, providing high-quality products and services, and consistently delivering on promises.

Furthermore, the drug cartels often operate outside the law, and this illegal activity often leads to their downfall. Entrepreneurs should always operate within the legal framework and avoid any illegal or unethical practices.

In conclusion, while the physical prowess and weapon mastery of drug lords may seem excessive, it serves as a reminder of the cutthroat nature of the drug industry and the importance of being well-rounded and capable in all aspects of business. As an entrepreneur, it is crucial to have a deep understanding and mastery of the core technical skills that drive your industry, and to take responsibility for continuously improving upon these skills. Additionally, it's important to operate within the legal framework and to focus on building a strong reputation and fostering trust with customers, employees and partners.

CHAPTER 2

ALWAYS HAVE A PLAN (DRUG LORDS NEVER GO TO A BUSINESS DEAL WITHOUT A PLAN B)

DRUG lords are often seen as ruthless and violent criminals who operate outside of the law. However, one aspect of their operations that is often overlooked is their ability to plan and strategize. In order to survive and thrive in the highly competitive and dangerous world of drug trafficking, drug lords must be able to think ahead and anticipate potential problems. This is why the ability to plan is considered one of the top skills for drug lords.

One of the most important aspects of a drug

lord's plan is their ability to escape when the police come chasing. This requires a detailed understanding of the local area, including the layout of the streets and the location of potential hideouts. Drug lords also need to have a plan in place for how to move the money they earn securely, as they are often targeted by other criminals and law enforcement officers.

Another important aspect of a drug lord's plan is how to close a deal and leave the scene without getting short or held ransom. This requires a high level of negotiation skills and the ability to read people and situations. A drug lord must be able to identify potential threats and take action to protect themselves and their assets.

It is not just drug lords that require planning skills to be successful, but also business leaders and entrepreneurs. A business leader and entrepreneur cannot successfully build a business without planning skills. From planning product launch, to marketing to operations, to daily plans to yearly plan and more, planning is critical for success in business the same like it is important for drug lord. If you are thinking of starting a business, having a business plan will greatly help you, having a startup action plan will help you and more.

When developing a business plan, it is important to consider the following:

Market research: Understand your target market, their needs, and how your product or service will meet those needs.

Financial projections: Develop a financial plan that includes projected income, expenses, and profits. This will help you to identify potential financial pitfalls and make adjustments accordingly.

Competitive analysis: Understand your competition and what sets your business apart from them.

Marketing strategies: Develop a marketing plan that will help you reach your target market and generate leads.

Operations plan: Determine how your business will function on a day-to-day basis, including inventory management, staffing, and procedures.

Plan B: Prepare for potential challenges and have a backup plan in place in case things don't go as planned.

A comprehensive business plan is a blueprint for your business, outlining your goals, strategies, and actions. It should include market research, financial projections, and a detailed analysis of your competition. A business plan also serves as a roadmap for your business, guiding you in making important decisions and staying on track to achieve your goals.

In conclusion, while it may seem counterintuitive, drug lords and successful business leaders have a lot in common when it comes to planning. Both require a high level of strategic thinking and the ability to anticipate potential problems. By taking a page out of the drug lord's playbook and always having a plan, business leaders and entrepreneurs can increase their chances of success.

CHAPTER 3

HUNT FOR INFORMATION

AS depicted in movies and documentaries, one of the defining characteristics of successful drug lords is their ability to gather and utilize information.

Whether it's about their competitors, potential threats, or law enforcement efforts, drug lords are constantly on the hunt for information that can help them protect and grow their operations. This is because they understand that information is one of the most critical elements in running a successful drug ring or cartel.

In the world of drug trafficking, having access to the right information can mean the difference between success and failure. This is why drug lords are willing to pay large sums of money to acquire information, no matter how small or insignificant it may seem. They understand that even the smallest piece of information can have a significant impact on their operations, whether it's in the realm of drug manufacturing, packaging, transportation, delivery, or moving money.

This same principle applies to the business world. In order to start and run a successful business, entrepreneurs must also be on the hunt for information. This includes researching the market, validating their product or service, analyzing competitors, gathering economic data, understanding tax and finance laws, and staying informed about regulations in their industry. Without this information, entrepreneurs may find themselves at a disadvantage and struggling to compete.

One of the key elements in hunting for information is conducting market research. This involves gathering data about your target market, including their needs, wants, and pain points. This information will help you understand what your customers want and how your product or service can meet their needs.

Another important aspect is conducting competitive analysis. This involves researching your competitors, including their strengths, weaknesses, and strategies. This information will help you understand how to differentiate your product or service and position it in the market.

In addition, entrepreneurs must stay

informed about the economic climate and laws and regulations that can impact their business. This includes understanding tax laws, finance regulations, and other industry-specific regulations. This will ensure that they are in compliance with legal requirements and can make informed decisions about their business operations.

In conclusion, information is key in the world of drug trafficking and business. Successful drug lords and entrepreneurs understand the importance of hunting for information and using it to their advantage. By gathering the right information and data, entrepreneurs can make informed decisions and stay ahead of the competition. The hunt for information is an ongoing process, and it is necessary for entrepreneurs to continually gather and analyze information to stay competitive and make strategic decisions for the growth and success of their business.

CHAPTER 4

DRUG LORDS THINK LONG TERM

DRUG lords, despite the high risks and uncertainty of their business, are known for their ability to think long term. They understand that in order to succeed in the drug trafficking world, they must plan and manage their operations with the future in mind.

This means investing in new routes, equipment, and relationships, as well as recruiting new members of the cartel, all in the pursuit of long-term dominance. This

15

ability to think ahead and plan for the future is a key characteristic of those who are able to thrive in the drug trafficking business.

This same principle applies to the business world. Entrepreneurs and executives must also think long-term, despite the challenges and risks they may face. It can be easy to get caught up in the day-to-day challenges of running a business, but it's important to remember that the future is what matters most.

For example, even if the business is going through a tough time, the entrepreneur should not neglect future possibilities and opportunities. They should keep in mind that the challenges are temporary and that it will pass. In the meantime, they should continue to invest in the business, look for new opportunities, and plan for the future.

An entrepreneur should also have a vision for

the future, a long-term goal for the business. They should have a plan for how to achieve that goal, and they should work towards it every day. This vision should be communicated to everyone in the organization, and everyone should work towards achieving it together.

In addition, entrepreneurs should also consider the future trends and changes in the market and industry. They should anticipate what the future holds and plan accordingly. They should invest in new technologies, products or services that will be in demand in the future. This will help them to stay ahead of the curve and be prepared for the future.

In summation, drug lords and entrepreneurs alike understand the importance of thinking long-term. Despite the risks and challenges they may face, they believe in their ability to succeed and plan for the future.

Entrepreneurs should remember that although the present is important, the future is what matters most, and they should take actions in the present day with the future in mind. A visionary entrepreneur who can think long-term, despite the challenges, is more likely to succeed in their business.

CHAPTER 5

DRUG LORDS SET EMPLOYEE POLICIES & ARE FIRM IN RESPECTING THEM

TRUTH is, drug lords, in order to maintain control and discipline within their organizations, often have strict policies in place and are firm in enforcing them. This includes severe consequences for disloyalty or betrayal, as well as for actions that go against the code of the cartel. For drug lords, it is not about emotions, but rather about maintaining the integrity of the organization and preserving the authority of the leader.

This same principle applies to the business world, as well. A company's success depends on the actions of its employees, and it is important for leaders to establish clear policies and ensure that they are respected. This includes having a staff handbook and policy manual in place, and making sure that the team is aware of the policies and the consequences for not respecting them.

One key aspect of setting employee policies is to clearly define the expectations and responsibilities of each employee, and to be consistent in enforcing them. This includes setting guidelines for performance, attendance, and conduct, as well as consequences for not meeting these expectations.

Additionally, it is important for leaders to communicate the policies clearly and make sure that all employees understand them, as well as the consequences for not following them.

Another important aspect is to be firm in

enforcing the policies and taking appropriate actions when an employee goes against them. This sends a clear message to the rest of the team that the policies are not to be taken lightly and that the leader is serious about maintaining discipline and control. It also helps to establish a culture of respect and accountability within the organization.

Moreover, it is important to have a process in place to address and resolve conflicts that may arise due to the policies, and to ensure that the employees are aware of the process. This can include having a designated person or team to handle complaints and grievances, and to provide employees with a clear understanding of the steps that will be taken to resolve the situation.

This is to say, drug lords and business leaders alike understand the importance of having clear policies in place and being firm in enforcing them. This is necessary in order to maintain control and discipline within the organization, and to establish a culture of respect and accountability.

By setting clear policies and being consistent in enforcing them, leaders can ensure that the organization runs smoothly and that the team is focused on achieving common goals. Additionally, by having a process in place to resolve conflicts, leaders can create a positive and peaceful environment for the team.

CHAPTER 6

DRUG CARTEL LORDS BUILD STRONG RELATIONSHIPS WITH CORE STAKEHOLDERS

DRUG cartel lords are known for their ability to build strong relationships with key stakeholders. They understand that in order to be successful in the drug trafficking business, they must have support from key players in their network, including court officials, law enforcement officers, politicians, community leaders, and other drug lords.

In order to gain this support, they will use a variety of tactics, including bribery, threats, gifts, and even marriage proposals. Building strong relationships is a critical component of their operations, and they will go to great lengths to maintain these relationships.

This same principle applies to the business world. Entrepreneurs and business leaders must also understand the importance of building strong relationships with key stakeholders. These relationships can include those with suppliers, partners, customers, bank managers, investors, and other people of influence within the community or industry.

One key aspect of building relationships is to identify who the key stakeholders are, and to understand their needs, goals and motivations. This will help entrepreneurs to tailor their approach and to establish a mutually beneficial relationship. Entrepreneurs should also invest in building relationships that align with the business goals, and that can help them to achieve their objectives.

Another important aspect is to be ethical in building relationships. Entrepreneurs should avoid using unethical tactics such as bribery, fraud or any other illegal activities to gain support. Instead, they should focus on building genuine relationships that are based on trust, integrity and mutual respect. Building relationships that will hurt the business in the long run should be avoided.

Additionally, entrepreneurs should also invest in maintaining and nurturing their relationships. This means staying in touch with key stakeholders, keeping them informed about the business, and actively seeking their input and feedback. It also means being responsive to their needs and addressing any issues or concerns that may arise. By actively maintaining and nurturing their relationships, entrepreneurs can ensure that they remain strong and continue to be beneficial for both parties.

Another way to build strong relationships is through networking. Entrepreneurs should attend industry events, conferences, and networking groups to meet and connect with other business leaders and potential partners. This can help them to establish new relationships and to expand their network of contacts. They should also leverage social media and digital platforms to connect with potential partners and stakeholders.

In all, drug cartel lords understand the importance of building strong relationships with key stakeholders. This is a critical component of their operations, and they will go to great lengths to maintain these relationships. The same principle applies to the business world, entrepreneurs must also understand the importance of building strong relationships with key stakeholders. This includes identifying key stakeholders, understanding their needs and goals, being ethical in building relationships, nurturing and maintaining relationships and networking.

By building strong relationships with key stakeholders, entrepreneurs can ensure that their business operations are supported and can thrive.

CHAPTER 7

DRUG CARTEL LORDS ALWAYS HAVE A SECRET MOVE

IN a drug cartel movie I watched few years back, a lord mentioned one of his secrets to his close collaborator. According to him, that one thing he knew (which no one else knew) is what has kept him in the business for decades. He obliged this too collaborator never to reveal it to anyone. This scene sparked my curiosity on the importance of secrets and sacred Information.

Drug cartel lords are known for always having a secret move, something that only they know about and that can serve as a backup plan in case things go wrong. This could be anything from a secret lawyer or bank account, to a secret escape plan or even a secret hideout in a remote location.

This strategy is a smart one, as it allows them to be prepared for any eventuality and to protect themselves and their operations from potential betrayals or threats.

This same principle can also apply to the business world. However, unlike drug cartel lords, legal businesses can and should share their secret moves with key members of their team, particularly in cases of succession planning. This is because having a secret move can give a business a competitive advantage in the marketplace, positioning them ahead of their competition.

For example, a business can have a secret move like the launch of a new product in a few months or years, which can take the competition by surprise. Another secret move could be an expansion move to another country, which can give the business access to new markets and customers. Or it could be a secret move to acquire a smaller competitor, which can give the business a larger market share. Or it could be serve business bank account with reserve funds for rainy days.

It is important to note that in business, secret moves should be kept confidential and should not be shared with the public until the appropriate time, in order to maintain the element of surprise and to protect the business's competitive advantage.

This is what we mean: drug cartel lords always have a secret move that only they know, it's a strategy that allows them to be prepared for any eventuality and to protect themselves and their operations from potential betrayals or threats.

The same principle applies to the business

world, legal businesses should also have secret moves that can give them a competitive advantage in the marketplace, positioning them ahead of their competition. Secret moves should be kept confidential, and it is important to share it with the top team management leaders for the purpose of succession planning.

By Dr. Javnyuy Joybert

CHAPTER 8

DRUG CARTEL LORDS ARE LOGICALLY DRIVEN WITH HIGHEST LEVEL OF EMOTIONAL INTELLIGENCE

EMOTIONAL Intelligence is a top skill today. Drug cartel lords, known for their ability to run and manage illegal operations, are often portrayed as being highly emotionally intelligent individuals.

They are able to remain calm and logical in high-pressure situations, and are able to make decisions based on facts and evidence rather than emotions. They understand the importance of keeping their emotions in check, and are able to avoid letting emotions cloud their judgment. This allows them to make rational and calculated decisions that are in the best interest of their business

32

By Dr. Javnyuy Joybert

operations.

This same principle applies to the business world, where emotional intelligence is a critical element for success. A business leader who is able to manage their own emotions, as well as the emotions of others, is more likely to succeed. They are able to lead their team with empathy, compassion and logic and not let emotions cloud their judgement.

They are able to build and maintain relevant relationships with customers, team members, and other stakeholders and make decisions that are in the best interest of the business.

Emotional Intelligence is a skill that can be developed, and entrepreneurs should invest time and effort in building their emotional intelligence. This could include things like learning how to manage stress, understanding how to read and respond to the emotions of others, and learning how to communicate effectively.

In addition, Emotional Intelligence is not only important in day-to-day operations but also in crisis management. A leader with high emotional intelligence will be able to remain calm and composed in difficult situations, and will be able to make decisions that are in the best interest of the business, employees and stakeholders.

The long and short of this chapter is: drug cartel lords are known for their ability to remain logically driven and emotionally intelligent in high-pressure situations. This same principle applies to the business world, where emotional intelligence is a critical element for success.

Entrepreneurs should invest time and effort in building their emotional intelligence, as it can help them to lead their team with empathy, compassion and logic, to build and maintain relevant relationships with customers and stakeholders and to make decisions that are in the best interest of the business.

By Dr. Javnyuy Joybert

CHAPTER 9

DRUG CARTEL LORDS BUILD ALLIANCE IN OTHER TO PENETRATE NEW MARKETS

NEW market penetration strategies are like oil to an engine in the entrepreneurial world. Drug cartel lords are known for their ability to build alliances in order to penetrate new markets. They understand that it can be costly and time-consuming to enter a new market, and that building an alliance with another cartel that already has a presence in that market can greatly benefit their operations. For example, a drug cartel in South America may enter an alliance with a drug cartel in Eastern Europe in order to penetrate the market with their new product. This allows them to leverage the existing resources and network of the other cartel, which can save them time and money and help them to establish a foothold in the new market.

This same principle applies to the business world. Entrepreneurs and business leaders who are looking to penetrate new markets in other countries or continents should consider building alliances with other businesses that already have a presence in those markets. This can be a cost-effective and efficient way to enter a new market, as the business can leverage the resources and network of the other business, which can help them to establish a foothold and grow their operations.

Building alliances can come in different forms, it could be a joint venture, strategic partnership, merger or acquisition and more. A joint venture is a partnership between two or more businesses to share resources, skills, and knowledge to achieve a common goal. A strategic partnership is a relationship between two or more businesses to share resources, skills, and knowledge to achieve a common goal. A merger is the combination of two or more businesses into one, and an acquisition is the purchase of one business by another.

For example, a business that specializes in manufacturing eco-friendly products may enter into a strategic partnership with a business that specializes in sustainable packaging in order to penetrate the market for eco-friendly products in another country or continent. The business that specializes in sustainable packaging can leverage their existing resources and network to help the other business establish a foothold in the new market.

By Dr. Javnyuy Joybert

In addition to alliances, businesses can also enter new markets by acquiring or merging with local companies. This can provide a quick and efficient way to enter a new market, as the business can leverage the existing resources, network, and market knowledge of the local company.

In conclusion, drug cartel lords are experts at building alliances in order to penetrate new markets. They understand the benefits of working with other cartels that already have a presence in those markets and can leverage their resources, network and market knowledge.

This same principle applies to the business world, where entrepreneurs and business leaders should consider building alliances, joint ventures, strategic partnership, merger or acquisition with other businesses that

39

already have a presence in new markets to save costs and time, and to grow their operations. Building alliances, joint ventures, strategic partnership, merger or acquisition can be a cost-effective and efficient way to enter new markets and achieve greater profit.

CHAPTER 10

DRUG CARTEL LORDS HAVE THE MENTALITY TO DOMINATE THE MARKETS

DOMINATION is for winners; competition is for losers. Drug cartel lords are known for their ruthless mindset to dominate their market. They have the attitude and mindset to win the entire market, and to eliminate any competition that may stand in their way. They do not believe in small-mindedness or thinking small, even if they are starting small. They have big dreams to expand and expand to the whole region, country, continent, and even the world.

This mindset, referred to as the dominance mentality, is a critical lesson that

41

entrepreneurs can learn from drug lords. As an entrepreneur, it's important to have a long-term vision for your business and to always strive for growth and expansion. Even if you're starting small, you should aim for the global market, and develop strategies to take over your local market first, then your region, country, continent and even the world.

Having a dominance mentality will challenge you to act in ways that will set you up for success. Entrepreneurs should focus on building a strong brand, creating a competitive advantage, and continuously innovating to stay ahead of the competition.

Furthermore, entrepreneurs should aim to create a diverse portfolio of products and services, and to diversify their revenue streams. This will reduce the risk of relying on one product or service and increase their chances of long-term success. Additionally, they should look for opportunities to enter new markets, whether through partnerships, joint ventures, or acquisitions.

In conclusion, drug cartel lords have a mindset to dominate their market, which entrepreneurs can learn from. Entrepreneurs should aim big and strive to dominate their market. They should have a long-term vision for growth and expansion, and strive to continuously innovate and diversify their products and revenue streams. They should also aim to enter new markets through partnerships, joint ventures, or acquisitions, and always aim for global expansion. This mindset is essential for entrepreneurs to achieve long-term success in the business world.

Before we go to the next chapter let me

highlight some core mindset every successful entrepreneur must develop:

<u>Growth mindset:</u> This mindset is the belief that one's abilities and intelligence can be developed through hard work, effort, and learning. Entrepreneurs who possess a growth mindset are more likely to take risks, persevere through challenges, and continuously improve their skills and knowledge.

<u>Resilience mindset:</u> This mindset is the ability to bounce back from setbacks and challenges. Entrepreneurs with a resilience mindset possess the ability to handle stress and pressure, and to remain optimistic even in difficult situations. They are able to take a step back, reassess the situation, and come up with a new plan of action.

Creativity mindset: This mindset is the ability to think outside the box and come up with new and innovative ideas. Entrepreneurs who possess a creativity mindset are able to identify new opportunities, solve problems in unique ways, and develop new products or services.

Adaptability mindset: This mindset is the ability to change and adapt to new situations and environments. Entrepreneurs who possess an adaptability mindset are able to quickly react to changes in the market, and pivot their business strategy as needed.

Risk-taking mindset: This mindset is the willingness to take calculated risks in order to achieve success. Entrepreneurs who possess a risk-taking mindset are willing to take bold actions and make bold decisions in order to achieve their goals, even if it means taking on a certain level of risk.

CHAPTER 11

DRUG CARTEL LORDS INTENTIONALLY HIRE SMART TALENTS FOR GROWTH PURPOSES

TALENTS make businesses potent.

This cannot be overemphasized. Take for example, Drug cartel lords are known for their ruthless mindset to dominate their market, and part of that strategy is to intentionally hire smart talents for growth purposes. They understand that the smartest talents play a key role in running smooth and profitable operations. They are aware that they cannot hire average performers and expect great business results.

I am a big fan of F&F. In the fast and furious franchise movie, a drug cartel lord organized a driving competition to select and hire the 2 best drivers to move his drugs from South America to the USA market. In other movies, we have seen drug cartel lords hire the best snipers, the best combat fighters, the best hackers, and more, all for the sake of their operations.

This same principle applies in business. Companies such as Google, Apple, Microsoft, Facebook, and other great companies invest in recruiting the best and smartest talents they can get. They know that a company will never grow above the quality of the talents working for the business. As an entrepreneur and business executive, it is crucial to establish a plan on how you will hire, keep, and grow the smartest talents in your business.

To attract and retain the best talents, entrepreneurs should focus on building a strong company culture that values innovation, creativity, and continuous learning. They should also provide competitive compensation packages, benefits, and opportunities for growth and development.

Furthermore, entrepreneurs should invest in training and development programs for their employees, and provide them with the necessary tools and resources to excel in their roles. This will not only help employees to improve their skills but also increase their motivation and engagement.

Additionally, entrepreneurs should also consider hiring diverse talents with different backgrounds, skills, and perspectives to bring in fresh ideas and new perspectives to the company. This will foster a more inclusive and innovative work environment.

Matter-of-factly, drug cartel lords understand the importance of hiring smart talents in order to achieve growth and success in their operations. Entrepreneurs should also adopt this mindset and focus on intentionally hiring the best and smartest talents for their business. This includes building a strong company culture, providing competitive compensation and benefits, investing in training and development programs, and promoting diversity in the workplace. By focusing on attracting and retaining the best talents, entrepreneurs can set their business up for long-term growth and success.

CHAPTER 12

DRUG LORD CARTELS WILL GO TO ANY LENGTH TO PROTECT THEIR TERRITORY AND MARKET

DRUG cartel lords will go to any length to protect their territory and market, and this is evident from the numerous documentaries and movies that depict cartel wars over drug-selling territories. These battles can be violent and bloody, with rival cartels fighting for control over specific areas.

In business, the battle for territory and market share may not be as physical as it is in the drug cartels where they use guns, axes, machettes, mortal combats and others. However, it is still intense and requires strategic planning.

Entrepreneurs must take proactive measures to protect their territory and market share. This can be done by carrying out intensive marketing and sales campaigns, providing exceptional customer service, establishing customer loyalty programs, signing exclusive distribution deals, and implementing any other legal strategy or action that can protect the market.

One effective way to protect your market share is to focus on building a strong brand. A strong brand can differentiate you from your competitors and make it harder for them to enter your market. This can be done by creating a unique value proposition, developing a consistent brand identity, and building a loyal customer base.

Another way to protect your market share is to focus on innovation. By constantly developing new products or services and improving existing ones, you can stay ahead of the competition and maintain your market position. This can be done by conducting market research, gathering customer feedback, and investing in research and development.

Entrepreneurs should also focus on building strategic partnerships and alliances. By forming strategic partnerships with other companies, you can expand your reach and access new markets. This can be done by identifying complementary companies, building relationships, and identifying areas where you can collaborate.

In addition, entrepreneurs should also focus on building a strong online presence. By having a strong online presence, entrepreneurs can reach a wider audience and attract new customers. This can be done by building a website, creating social media accounts, and investing in search engine optimization (SEO) and pay-per-click (PPC) advertising.

Finally, entrepreneurs should also focus on building a strong team. By hiring the right people, entrepreneurs can build a team that is dedicated and capable of achieving their goals. This can be done by identifying the right skills, recruiting top talent, and investing in training and development programs.

This means, drug cartel lords will go to any length to protect their territory and market, and entrepreneurs should also adopt this mindset in order to protect their market share and maintain their position in the industry. By focusing on building a strong brand, innovating, forming strategic partnerships, building a strong online presence, and building a strong team, entrepreneurs can protect their market share and set their business up for long-term success.

Additionally, entrepreneurs should stay abreast of the laws, regulations and industry trends in order to ensure compliance and stay competitive. Furthermore, entrepreneurs should be prepared to adapt to changing market conditions, be able to pivot and make strategic decisions to maintain their competitive edge.

CHAPTER 13

DRUG CARTEL LORDS TACTFULLY IDENTIFY AND KNOW THE WEAK POINT OF THEIR COMPETITOR (ENEMY)

IN the world of drug cartels, identifying and exploiting the weak points of one's competitors and enemies is a crucial strategy for achieving success.

However, while the methods employed by drug lords may be illegal and unethical, the underlying principle of identifying and exploiting weaknesses can also be applied in a legal and ethical manner within the business world.

As a business leader, it is important to

56

conduct thorough competitor analysis in order to identify gaps in the market and opportunities for growth.

For example, if a competitor is weak in their packaging design, a business leader can take advantage of this weakness by investing in more visually appealing packaging for their own products. Similarly, if a competitor is struggling with their marketing strategy, a business leader can take advantage of this weakness by developing a more effective marketing plan for their own company.

In addition to identifying and exploiting weaknesses in competitors, it is also important for business leaders to be aware of the weak points of key stakeholders, such as customers and suppliers. By understanding these weaknesses, a business leader can take steps to mitigate potential risks and use these weaknesses to their advantage when necessary. For example, if a key supplier is dependent on a single source of raw materials, a business leader can use this information to negotiate better prices or secure alternative sources of materials.

While the methods employed by drug lords may be extreme and illegal, the principle of identifying and exploiting weaknesses is a valuable tool for any business leader looking to gain a competitive edge. By tactfully identifying and exploiting the weak points of competitors and key stakeholders, a business leader can create opportunities for growth and increase their chances of success in the market.

Another important aspect to consider when identifying the weaknesses of competitors is understanding how they operate. For example, if a competitor heavily relies on a single product or service, a business leader can focus on diversifying their own offerings to mitigate the impact of any potential disruption to that product or service. Additionally, understanding a competitor's supply chain and logistics can also provide valuable insight into potential vulnerabilities.

Furthermore, it's not only about identifying the weaknesses of competitors, but also about understanding the strengths of competitors. By understanding what makes a competitor successful, a business leader can learn valuable lessons and apply them to their own business. For example, if a competitor has a strong brand image, a business leader can focus on building their own brand and creating a strong identity for their company.

Moreover, it's also important to keep track of the trends in the industry and the market, by doing so, business leaders will be able to identify the potential weaknesses of the competitors and take advantage of them. For example, if a trend of sustainable products is gaining popularity and a competitor is not following the trend, a business leader can take advantage of this by introducing sustainable products to their own line.

Conclusively, the drug cartel lords tactfully identify and know the weak point of their competitor (enemy) and use them to their advantage. Business leaders can also use this principle in a legal and ethical manner by conducting thorough competitor analysis and identifying opportunities for growth.

By tactfully identifying and exploiting the weak points of competitors and key stakeholders, a business leader can create opportunities for growth and increase their chances of success in the market. It's important to understand not only the weaknesses but also the strengths of the competitors, as well as keeping track of the industry trends to stay ahead in the game.

CHAPTER 14

DRUG CARTEL LORDS KNOW THEIR GREATEST PITFALL AND HAVE A PLAN

LORDS of drug cartel are well aware that getting arrested and going to prison are their greatest pitfalls. They understand that law enforcement agencies and the criminal justice system are constantly on the lookout for them, and that they could be apprehended at any moment.

This awareness drives them to always have a plan "B" in place. This could be an escape plan when the police come, a plan to bribe a judge, or a plan to gain favor from the prison chief. The point is, they always have a plan.

As entrepreneurs and business executives, it

is important to adopt this same mindset. In business, there are always potential pitfalls that must be considered. These could include poor sales, being pushed out of the market by competitors, or going out of business because of poor strategies. It is the responsibility of the entrepreneur and executive to identify these potential pitfalls and have a plan in place to mitigate or overcome them.

One way to identify and plan for potential pitfalls is by conducting a SWOT analysis. SWOT analysis is a tool that helps identify a company's strengths, weaknesses, opportunities, and threats. By identifying these areas, entrepreneurs and business executives can develop strategies to mitigate potential risks and capitalize on opportunities. This can be done by creating a plan for poor sales, such as increasing marketing efforts or diversifying product offerings. A plan for competitors pushing a business out of the market could include investing in research and development to create a more innovative product or service.

Another effective way to identify and plan for potential pitfalls is by conducting a scenario planning. This process involves identifying possible future outcomes and developing strategies to address them. This allows entrepreneurs and business executives to anticipate potential risks and challenges and prepare for them in advance. By doing so, they can be more resilient and adaptable in the face of adversity.

It's also important to have an emergency fund, this fund can help mitigate some of the financial impact of a pitfall. For example, a business leader can use emergency funds to keep the business running while they work to address a poor sales problem.

Moreover, it's also essential to have a team of advisors and mentors. These people can offer valuable insights and advice on how to navigate potential pitfalls and provide support when things get tough. By having a support system in place, entrepreneurs and business executives can feel more confident and secure in their ability to overcome obstacles.

These drug cartel lords are aware of their greatest pitfall and have a plan. This is a valuable mindset for entrepreneurs and business executives to adopt. By identifying potential pitfalls and having a plan in place, entrepreneurs and business executives can be more resilient and adaptable in the face of adversity.

It's important to conduct a SWOT analysis

and scenario planning, have an emergency fund and have a team of advisors and mentors. By being proactive and intentional, entrepreneurs and business executives can minimize the impact of potential risks and capitalize on opportunities for growth and success.

Here is how you can conduct a SWOT analysis:

Conducting a SWOT analysis is an effective way for entrepreneurs to identify their company's strengths, weaknesses, opportunities, and threats.

Here is a practical step-by-step process for conducting a SWOT analysis:

Gather information: Begin by gathering information about your company, the industry, and the market. This includes financial data, customer feedback, and information about your competitors.

Identify strengths: Look at your company's internal factors and determine what sets you apart from your competitors. These are your strengths. Examples of strengths include a strong brand, a loyal customer base, or a proprietary technology.

Identify weaknesses: Identify internal factors that are holding your company back. These are your weaknesses. Examples of weaknesses include a lack of resources, poor management, or a weak product line.

Identify opportunities: Look at external factors and identify potential opportunities for growth. These are external opportunities.

Examples of opportunities include a new market, a change in consumer behavior, or a technological advancement.

Identify threats: Identify external factors that could harm your business. These are your threats. Examples of threats include a recession, new competitors, or a change in government regulations.

Prioritize: Prioritize the identified strengths, weaknesses, opportunities, and threats based on their potential impact on your business.

Create an action plan: After identifying and prioritizing the SWOT elements, create an action plan to address each area. For strengths, develop ways to maximize and leverage them. For weaknesses, develop ways to mitigate or eliminate them. For opportunities, develop ways to capitalize on them. For threats, develop ways to prepare for them or reduce their impact.

Monitor and review: Regularly monitor and review the SWOT analysis to see if your action plan is working or if there are any new strengths, weaknesses, opportunities, or threats that have emerged.

By following this process, entrepreneurs can gain a better understanding of their company's current situation and develop strategies to address potential risks and capitalize on opportunities for growth. It's important to involve different members of the company, like managers, employees and customers, to gather different perspectives and insights.

CHAPTER 15

DRUG CARTEL LORDS ARE WILLING TO TAKE THE NECESSARY RISK TO ENJOY THE BIG PAYCHECK

BUSINESS without risks only exist in fairy tales. Drug cartel lords are a prime example of individuals who understand the importance of taking calculated risks in order to achieve financial success. They possess a unique ability to analyze opportunities and determine whether the potential payoff justifies the risk involved.

However, it's important to note that these individuals aren't reckless in their decision making. They are selective in the opportunities they choose to pursue and only take the necessary risks that will have the greatest impact on their operations. This level of discernment is crucial in any business endeavor.

Entrepreneurs and business executives can learn a valuable lesson from the actions of drug cartel lords in this regard. To grow a business, one must be willing to take the necessary risks that will push the company forward. This may include expanding into new markets, investing in new equipment, increasing inventory, and improving distribution channels.

But taking risks doesn't have to be limited to these traditional business strategies. Entrepreneurs can also get creative and think outside the box. For example, they could consider developing new and innovative products, or implementing unique marketing campaigns to attract customers.

Another practical idea could be to form strategic partnerships with other companies or invest in emerging technologies such as artificial intelligence, blockchain, and virtual reality to stay competitive in the market.

Drug cartel lords serve as a reminder that taking risks is a necessary component of achieving success in business. Entrepreneurs and business executives should not be afraid to step out of their comfort zones and take calculated risks in order to grow their companies and achieve financial success. With a combination of calculated risk-taking, creativity and innovative thinking, the sky is the limit for any business.

Step by step process an entrepreneur should go through to take calculated risk:

<u>Identify the potential opportunity:</u> The first step in taking a calculated risk is to identify potential opportunities that align with the

By Dr. Javnyuy Joybert

goals and objectives of the business. This could include expanding into new markets, launching a new product or service, or implementing new technology.

Conduct research and analysis: Before making any decisions, it's important to conduct thorough research and analysis on the potential opportunity. This includes researching the market, the competition, and identifying any potential risks and challenges.

Develop a risk management plan: Once you have a clear understanding of the opportunity and the potential risks involved, develop a risk management plan to mitigate any potential negative impacts. This could include setting up contingencies and backup plans in case things don't go as expected.

Assess the potential rewards: Consider the potential rewards of taking the risk and how they align with the goals and objectives of the business. This includes an assessment of the financial, strategic and reputational benefits of the opportunity.

Make the decision: Based on the research, analysis, risk management plan and the potential rewards, make the decision on whether to move forward with the opportunity.

Implement the plan: Once the decision is made, implement the plan and closely monitor progress. Be prepared to make adjustments as necessary and be willing to pivot if necessary.

Review and evaluate: After the plan has been

implemented, review and evaluate the results. This includes assessing the impact on the business, any lessons learned and how to apply them in the future.

Continuously monitor the environment for new opportunities: Keep an eye out for new opportunities and be prepared to take calculated risks when the time is right. Continuously monitor the market, competition and the environment for new opportunities.

It's important to note that taking calculated risks is not a one-time event, it's an ongoing process that requires continuous monitoring and adaptation. Entrepreneurs should always be on the lookout for new opportunities and be willing to take calculated risks to grow their business and achieve success.

CHAPTER 16

DRUG LORDS DETACH THEMSELVES FROM A FAILED DEAL AND MOVE TO THE NEXT ONE

DRUG cartel lords are known for their ability to detach themselves from failed deals and quickly move on to the next opportunity. They understand that failure is a natural part of business and that dwelling on a setback will only hinder their ability to succeed in the future.

While it's true that a failed deal can result in financial losses and logistical challenges, drug cartel lords do not let these setbacks discourage them. Instead, they take the lessons learned from the failure and use them to make the next deal more successful. This resilience and determination is a key trait that entrepreneurs and business executives can learn from.

Entrepreneurship is a journey filled with many ups and downs. It's important to be able to handle the setbacks, learn from them and move forward with a positive attitude. Entrepreneurs who are able to detach themselves from a failed deal and move on to the next opportunity with a resilient mindset are more likely to succeed in the long run.

One way to move forward from a failed deal is to reflect on what went wrong and identify areas for improvement. This could include refining the business model, improving customer service, or finding more efficient ways to operate. Reflecting on the failure and understanding the reasons behind it can help entrepreneurs to create a plan for the next deal, this way they can avoid making the same mistakes.

Another practical idea for entrepreneurs to detach themselves from a failed deal and move to the next one is to seek mentorship and guidance from experienced entrepreneurs who have been through similar setbacks. This can provide valuable perspective and new ideas for tackling future opportunities.

Entrepreneurs can also take a break, take a step back and focus on their physical, mental and emotional well-being. Failure can take a toll on an entrepreneur's mental and emotional well-being, so it's important to take care of oneself before moving on to the next opportunity. Taking a break, practicing mindfulness and engaging in self-care activities can help entrepreneurs to recharge and gain a fresh perspective on the next opportunity.

In conclusion, drug cartel lords serve as a valuable example of how to detach oneself from a failed deal and move on to the next opportunity. Entrepreneurs and business executives can learn from this mindset, and take practical steps to detach themselves from failed deals, learn from them and move forward with a resilient mindset. With a positive attitude and a determination to succeed, entrepreneurs can turn failure into an opportunity to learn, grow, and ultimately achieve success.

Step by step process an entrepreneur can follow to overcome failure and move forward:

Acknowledge the failure: The first step in moving forward from failure is to acknowledge that it has occurred. Avoiding or denying the reality of the failure will only prolong the process of moving on.

Reflect on the failure: Take time to reflect on the failure and examine the events that led up to it. Consider what went wrong and what could have been done differently.

Identify the lessons learned: Failure can be a valuable learning opportunity. Identify the lessons that can be learned from the failure and how they can be applied in the future.

Practice self-compassion: Be kind and understanding to yourself. Failure is a normal part of the entrepreneurial journey, and it's important to remember that everyone makes mistakes. Practice self-compassion and avoid self-criticism.

Seek support: Failure can be a lonely and isolating experience. Seek support from friends, family, or a therapist to process your emotions and gain perspective on the situation.

Practice mindfulness: Mindfulness can help entrepreneurs to detach themselves from failure, it can help to reduce stress, anxiety and negative thoughts related to the failure. Mindfulness practices such as meditation, yoga, and journaling can help entrepreneurs to focus on the present moment, and not dwelling on the past.

Set new goals: Failure can be an opportunity to re-evaluate your goals and set new ones. Identify new opportunities and set realistic and achievable goals that align with the lessons learned from the failure.

Take Action: Take action towards achieving your new goals, this can help entrepreneurs to move forward from the failure and to focus on the future.

Celebrate small successes: Failure can be a long process to move on from, celebrate small successes along the way, this can help entrepreneurs to keep motivated and see the progress they are making.

It's important to remember that *failure is a natural part of the entrepreneurial journey, and it's not a reflection of one's worth as a person.* Entrepreneurs should be kind to themselves and take the time to process the failure and learn from it. With the right mindset and a plan in place, entrepreneurs can move forward from failure and ultimately achieve success.

CHAPTER 17

DRUG CARTEL LORDS ARE INTENTIONAL ABOUT EFFICIENCY AND ROI

THEY are known for their intentional approach to efficiency and returns on investment (ROI) in their operations. They understand that in order to be successful, they must be constantly striving for efficiency and maximizing their ROI. This means paying close attention to all aspects of their operations and making sure that everything is running smoothly with no hiccups.

Entrepreneurs and business executives can learn a valuable lesson from this mindset. Intentionally leading a team with a focus on operations and efficiency is crucial for any business to grow and achieve success. A business that is not efficient and not intentionally driving growth and achieving ROI is likely to struggle in the market.

One practical idea for entrepreneurs to increase efficiency is to implement lean management principles. This could involve identifying and eliminating waste in processes, streamlining operations, and implementing just-in-time inventory management. This can help to reduce costs and increase productivity, resulting in improved efficiency and ROI.

Another practical idea is to invest in technology and automation. Technology can help to automate repetitive tasks, and increase the speed and accuracy of data processing, resulting in improved efficiency and ROI. Entrepreneurs can also invest in software and tools to help them manage their operations more efficiently.

Entrepreneurs can also look to outsource non-core operations to experts in the field. This can free up time and resources, allowing entrepreneurs to focus on their core competencies and increase efficiency and ROI.

In addition, entrepreneurs and business executives should be intentional about setting clear goals and measuring the performance of their operations. This could include setting targets for revenue, costs, and customer satisfaction. Measuring performance against these targets can help entrepreneurs to identify areas for improvement, and take action to increase efficiency and ROI.

In conclusion, drug cartel lords serve as a valuable example of how to be intentional about efficiency and ROI in operations. Entrepreneurs and business executives can learn from this mindset, and take practical steps to increase efficiency and ROI in their operations. With a focus on efficiency and ROI, entrepreneurs can position their businesses for success in the market.

By taking out time to learn, practice these biggest secrets of drug cartel lords, any entrepreneur Can establish a global brand that stands the test of time. See you on the top of your entrepreneurial journey.

Cheers,

Dr. Javnyuy Joybert

www.ingramcontent.com/pod-product-compliance
Lightning Source LLC
Chambersburg PA
CBHW070917220526
45467CB00004B/1441